The Spirit Hovers

The Spirit Hovers

Journeying through Chaos with Prayers

K. K. Yeo

CASCADE *Books* • Eugene, Oregon

THE SPIRIT HOVERS
Journeying through Chaos with Prayers

Cascade Books
An Imprint of Wipf and Stock Publishers
199 W. 8th Ave., Suite 3
Eugene, OR 97401
www.wipfandstock.com

ISBN 13: 978-1-61097-506-3

Cataloging-in-Publication data:

Yeo, Khiok-Khng.
The Spirit hovers : journeying through chaos with prayers / K. K. Yeo.

ISBN 13: 978-1-61097-506-3

xvi + 108 p.; 23 cm.

1. Prayers. 2. Bible—O.T.—Illustrations. 3. Aesthetics—Religious Aspects. I. Title.

BV245 Y46 2012

Manufactured in the USA.

CONTENTS

Journeying with Community—Being Sojourners

Journeying with Creation—*Shalom* of the Earth in Coexistence

Journeying with Empathy—The Priesthood of All Believers

Journeying to Wholeness—Bearers of the Good News

PREFACE

The Human Need

"IN THE BEGINNING WHEN God created the heavens and the earth, the earth was a formless void and darkness covered the face of the deep, while a wind from God swept over the face of the waters" (Gen 1:1–2).[1] The wind from God is the Spirit who hovers over chaos (symbolized by the waters)—void, formlessness, and meaninglessness. If the agent of creation is the Son, then the Spirit of God is the "mysterious yet irresistible" (*Siddur*) means of God's creating the cosmos. The word "hover" (*merachephet*) is used two other times in the Hebrew Scriptures: (1) to speak of an eagle offering caring protection and immanent empowerment of her young as she broods over them (in Deut 32:11: "as it spreads its wings, takes them up, and bears them aloft on its pinions"); (2) to speak of the agonizing shaking of one's inner being (such as a shaking in the bones) for the righteous word of God to transform the lives of his people (Jer 23:9). What a matrix of creation—and life itself—that we are being ushered into, this reality of breathing with God's Spirit despite the unformed abyss and lifeless chaos, because the Spirit can quicken and transform troubled waters into overflowing streams. Lord, by your wind/Spirit "the heavens were made fair" (Job 26:13), "from your lofty abode you water the mountains; the earth is satisfied with the fruit of your work" (Ps 104:13).

1. Unless otherwise noted, all Bible quotations are from the New Revised Standard Version.

Many of the Old Testament prayers included in this volume emerged from my time as interim dean at Garrett-Evangelical Theological Seminary, from January through June of 2003. Serving in the dean's office was profoundly challenging for me; not only was I required to be a *sicut-Deus* administrator who could perform all organizational tasks for the president, faculty, and students, but also I was called upon to be "superman," able to magically address a variety of problems and issues—both academic and personal. As a way of overcoming the dehumanizing effect the role had on me, I began to meditate on the books of Genesis, Exodus, Psalms, Isaiah, and Job—in part because I needed something new and energizing (I had prayed the New Testament more often than the Old), and in part because I hoped these prayers would keep me sane. I prayed to God unceasingly for wisdom and strength during this time, and these prayers did indeed bring me comfort, peace, and balance in the midst of a chaotic experience.

It is often crisis or weakness that gets us to bend our knees. Through prayer, any dilemma, challenge, or *problématique* can become fertile ground for growing in humanity as we journey with God, and consequently, sojourning with one another and with creation. Of all the prayers in the Old Testament, the most unlikely place to pray is from "the belly of the fish" (Jonah 2:1), yet the belly of the fish is where crisis resides. Abraham, in his trouble with Abimelech of Gerar, prays to God, and his prayer moves God to heal Abimelech and make his family prosperous (Gen 20:17). When faced with his wife's barrenness, Isaac prays to God, and Rebekah is able to conceive (Gen 25:21). Confronting an uncompromising opponent in the pharaoh, Moses prays to the Lord for strength and wisdom (Exod 8:30; 10:18); he prays as the Israelites anger God and God's fire burns them (Num 11:2); and he prays for forgiveness of the Israelites as they repent (Num 21:7). There is nothing standing between Moses and his God. He pleads and fasts and uses God's power to argue with God not to destroy the sinful and rebellious people at the foot of Mount Sinai where they worship the golden calf (Deuteronomy 9):

> Lord GOD, do not destroy the people who are your very own possession,
> whom you redeemed in your greatness,
> whom you brought out of Egypt with a mighty hand.

Remember your servants, Abraham, Isaac, and Jacob;
pay no attention to the stubbornness of this people,
their wickedness and their sin,
otherwise the land from which you have brought us might say,
'Because the LORD was not able to bring them into the land
that he promised them,
and because he hated them,
he has brought them out to let them die in the wilderness.'
For they are the people of your very own possession,
whom you brought out by your great power and by your
outstretched arm. (Deut 9:26–29)

Throughout the Old Testament, leaders, judges, and prophets pray in times of crisis. When the people ask for a king, rather than acknowledge God as King, the prophet Samuel prays to God (1 Sam 8:6). Facing his imminent death, King Hezekiah prays and weeps bitterly: "Remember now, O LORD, I implore you, how I have walked before you in faithfulness with a whole heart, and have done what is good in your sight" (2 Kgs 20:3). And Nehemiah prays to God for protection against his enemies (Neh 4:9).

Hope and the Effect of Prayers

Prayers allow us to court God and cultivate friendship with the Transcendent and Immanent One. From ancient times until today, friends of God have prayed to him. Job and Jonah, perhaps out of desperation, pray that their lives will be met with death sooner rather than later (Job 6:9; Jonah 4:3). They pray for what they know not, because there is nothing else they can do. Perhaps they are able to pray for the impossible precisely because they count on the grace and love of God that can work miracles.

Women and men all pray their hearts out. Women in the Old Testament weep bitterly (*e.g.*, Hannah in 1 Sam 1:10), not because God's response matches our distress, but because, what else can we do except pour out our hearts? Hannah believes that "for this child I prayed; and the LORD has granted me the petition that I made to him" (1 Sam 1:27). And then she leaps for joy, even before her prayer is answered, because the faithfulness of God is the ground of her faith: "My heart exults in the LORD; / my strength is exalted in my God. / My mouth derides my enemies, / because I rejoice in my victory" (1 Sam 2:1). Men likewise do the same: "Ezra prayed and made confession, weeping and throwing himself down before the house of God . . . The people also wept bitterly" (Ezra 10:1). King Hezekiah and the prophet Isaiah, son of Amoz, pray and cry to heaven (2 Chr 32:20). King David "wore sackcloth, . . . afflicted [him]self with fasting, [and] . . . prayed with head bowed on my bosom" (Ps 35:13). Jeremiah weeps and prays for his people (Jer 32).

The supreme lordship of God is always acknowledged by pious prophets in the Old Testament, and because of that, they dare to pray for the impossible. Jonah prays to the Lord:

> O LORD! Is not this what I said while I was still in my own country?
> That is why I fled to Tarshish at the beginning;
> for I knew that you are a gracious God and merciful,
> slow to anger, and abounding in steadfast love,
> and ready to relent from punishing. (Jonah 4:2)

The preamble to Hezekiah's prayer reveals his confidence: "O LORD, the God of Israel, who are enthroned above the cherubim, you are God, you alone, of all the kingdoms of the earth; you have made heaven and earth" (2 Kgs 19:15). As the Isaiah text narrates the threat from King Sennacherib of Assyria, Hezekiah's prayer is all the more urgent, and his reliance on God is unshakeable:

> O LORD the God of Israel,
> who are enthroned above the cherubim,
> you are God, you alone, of all the kingdoms of the earth;
> you have made heaven and earth.
> Incline your ear, O LORD, and hear;
> open your eyes, O LORD, and see;
> hear the words of Sennacherib,
> which he has sent to mock the living God.
> Truly, O LORD, the kings of Assyria have laid waste the nations and their lands,

> and have hurled their gods into the fire,
> though they were no gods,
> but the work of human hands—wood and stone—and so they were destroyed.
> So now, O LORD our God, save us, I pray you, from his hand,
> so that all the kingdoms of the earth may know that you, O LORD, are God alone. (2 Kgs 19:15–19)

Manasseh's entreaty and plea are heard by God, and Manasseh is restored; he knows then that "the LORD indeed was God" (2 Chr 33:13). Despite his many unanswered prayers, Job "prayed for his friends, and the LORD gave Job twice as much as he had before" (Job 42:10). On the basis of God's supremacy, Daniel is courageous enough to intercede and supplicate for the people in a long prayer, excerpted below:

> Ah, LORD, great and awesome God,
> keeping covenant and steadfast love
> with those who love you and keep your commandments,
> we have sinned and done wrong,
> acted wickedly and rebelled,
> turning aside from your commandments and ordinances.
> We have not listened to your servants the prophets,
> who spoke in your name to our kings, our princes, and our ancestors,
> and to all the people of the land.
> Righteousness is on your side, O LORD,
> but open shame, as at this day,
> falls on us, the people of Judah, the inhabitants of Jerusalem,
> and all Israel, those who are near and those who are far away,
> in all the lands to which you have driven them,
> because of the treachery that they have committed against you . . .

And now, O LORD our God,
who brought your people out of the land of Egypt
with a mighty hand and made your name renowned even to this day –
we have sinned, we have done wickedly.
O LORD, in view of all your righteous acts,
let your anger and wrath, we pray,
turn away from your city Jerusalem, your holy mountain;
because of our sins and the iniquities of our ancestors,
Jerusalem and your people have become a disgrace among all our neighbors.
Now therefore, O our God,
listen to the prayer of your servant and to his supplication,
and for your own sake, LORD, let your face shine upon your desolated sanctuary.
Incline your ear, O my God, and hear.
Open your eyes and look at our desolation and the city that bears your name.
We do not present our supplication before you on the ground of our righteousness,
but on the ground of your great mercies.
O LORD, hear; O LORD, forgive;
O LORD, listen and act and do not delay!
For your own sake, O my God,
because your city and your people bear your name!" (Dan 9: 4–7, 15–19)

The mystery of prayer in the Old Testament continues to be a mystery even today. We often say that sometimes God answers prayers, and sometimes he does not. And there may be a thousand reasons that prayers are not answered. Not all of Moses's, David's, and Job's prayers are answered. Job prays and prays, and yet still he is in pain and turmoil. David's psalms acknowledge that prayers are not manipulative means for human will to change the will of God; prayers are means of seeking God's mercies and glory. Moses often speaks to God face-to-face but his desire to enter the promised land is not granted. Yet we have examples of people in the

Old Testament whose prayers are answered—not because of their virtues or the logic of their prayers. Elisha prays to the Lord to open the eyes of the servant, and he immediately sees. The text describes a miraculous situation: "the mountain was full of horses and chariots of fire all around Elisha" (2 Kgs 6:17). Elisha's prayer also is very effective when he prays to the Lord to strike the Arameans with blindness (2 Kgs 6:18). The Lord adds fifteen more years to Hezekiah's life after he prays intensely (2 Kgs 20:4–6; 2 Chr 32:24). Hezekiah intercedes for the people of Ephraim, Manasseh, Issachar, and Zebulun for not cleansing themselves in accordance with the sanctuary's rules; God pardons them because, although unclean, they "set their hearts to seek God" (2 Chr 30:19).

How to Use This Prayer Book

The prayers collected here are personal and communal, representing more than just a particular juncture of my life; more broadly, they reflect the ways in which an individual constantly is reconnected to the community of saints (past, present, and future) for the wider reign of God's mercy and justice in the world. The vision of these prayers is to seek a union of the spiritual and the intellectual, leadership in the Christian community, ecumenical interaction, cross-cultural experience, personal and social transformation. Prayers serve to reconnect us to the community of one humanity as we seek to ground ourselves in the Source of all. Thus, I encourage you to be creative in using these prayers in your own prayer life (e.g., in the practice of centering prayer) and to feel free to change the words of the prayers so that they become your own. In public worship as well these prayers can be modified for the appropriate liturgical seasons or contexts.

It is in this spirit that I have invited readers as sojourners; we are all of us participating in a pilgrimage of walking humbly with God and awaiting his reign of justice and peace in the world. To help readers in using this collection of prayers, I have grouped them into thematic categories for easy reference: Journeying with God, Journeying with Community, Journeying with Creation, Journeying with Empathy, and Journeying to Wholeness. One way to use this book is to select the theme that most speaks to you and focus on the prayers in that section.

Another way to use this book is in conjunction with lectionary readings in either public worship or personal prayer. Scriptural notations are included throughout to allow readers to easily cross-reference the Scripture passage referred to in the prayer with the appropriate lectionary reading.

And finally, the prayers in this book can be adapted for congregational use in different parts of the order of worship—for the invocation, confession, benediction, and the like. Readers should feel free to use an excerpt from the (long) prayers included here or to combine two shorter prayers into one—and to include the prayer in the church worship bulletin (whether printed on paper or projected onto a screen).

I strongly encourage readers using these for personal prayer to focus on a primary theme or idea sparked by the prayer. The one- or two-line Bible verse that appears before each prayer is included to help readers remain centered in order to "pray without ceasing" (1 Thess 5:17) throughout the day. Likewise, if there is a verse or even a half verse in the prayer that speaks to you, you might reflect on it as you move into your daily activities. Because the Spirit breathes life into us as we breathe and pray, any line or phrase from these prayers also can be used as a "breath prayer" to recite at various times in your day. For me, songs and images are excellent media for helping me center myself to focus on the poetic justice of what God is doing in and through us for the sake of the world. None of these can contain the Spirit, for the Spirit prompts and moves us in ways beyond our understanding. It is important not to be too focused on results, for the journey itself has so much more surprise and joy than any "destination" we might imagine.

Slow down. Stay curious. And we will breathe the prayers of life.

Ash Wednesday
March 9, 2011

Journeying with God—
Beloved Children in Communion

In the Beginning

(Genesis 1)

"Let there be . . ." (Gen 1:3, 6, 14).

Dear Lord,
    when your children are too consumed with the instant now,
    help us to remember the beginning,
    so that our narrow vision
    might be healed by your creativity and power.
Help us to transform
    that which is "formless void and darkness"
    into meaningful existence and beauty
    through the power of your Holy Spirit.

When your children are too cynical about the future,
    help us to know the beginning
    that creates the future,

so that our vision and wonder
might be assured by your coming hope.
Help us to trust in you,
knowing that you are the God who raises the dead
and the God who creates out of nothing
all that is good, beautiful, and truthful.
Speak to us
so that we learn to embody your grace,
and view life in the present,
but live life towards the end. Amen!

You Are Heartbroken

(Genesis 3)

"But the LORD God called to the man, and said to him, 'Where are you?'" (Gen 3:9).

You created a garden for us,
    and charged us to be the gardeners,
    to plant seeds of hope,
    to tender flowers of faith,
    to water trees of love.
We love the beautiful bugs,
    the fruitful olives,
    the blushing bunnies,
    and your heart is content.
We wonder why the garden has a boundary,
    why the tree of the knowledge of good and evil is not for us,
    why the serpent is wise and crafty.
We wander, we wonder, we doubt;
    not knowing the pitfalls—
    we take the broad way of wanting to be divine.
We doubt, we begin to distrust your word;
    not knowing, we fall—
    we take the shameful path, becoming less than human.
And you, Friend, are brokenhearted,
    for we betray the mutual trust—
    we usurp your power and wisdom;
    by breaking your image of glory among us,
    we betray your love to us.

Forgive us,
    too fearful to walk with you anymore,
    so shameful that we hide from you,
    and too broken to honor our own kind and glorify you.
Yet, you seek us out,
    you cover us with sacrifices of your creation—
    your wounded heart bleeds for us.
Help us to trust your word,
    not as a law of unbending rules,
    but as a law of grace that leads to freedom, fullness, and possibility.
Help us to heed your commandment,
    a lifesaver that grants us communion with you in the security of your love.
Help us to be content with knowledge of goodness,
    not giving in to the temptation of knowing partially of evil.
For you have created us to be simple,
    in knowing you;
you have created us to be good,
    in trusting you;
you have created us in the speck of eternity,
    to walk with you—in the Garden of joy immaculate and love divine.
        Amen!

Here I Am, Lord

(Genesis 22)

"God said, 'Take your son, your only son Isaac,
whom you love . . . and offer him . . .'" (Gen 22:2).

Lord, "Here I am";
lead me not into temptation,
but to know we are your beloved.
"Here I am," Lord,
send me to your people to love them.
In being loved and in loving;
teach us to love you in obedience, whether we feel joyful or unwilling to obey,
but nevertheless with discipline.
In trial and testing that we always fail you,
we pray your grace is greater than our strength,
for the gift of your Beloved
is eternally more precious than our offerings.
In temptation, we always give in and sin against you,
we pray your love covers our weakness,
for your altar of forgiveness overshadows our faithlessness.

When you call us by name,
may we say, "Here I am, Lord."
When we hear your word of comfort,
may we rest in peace and stop the violence,
granting blessings to the vulnerable.

For we fear you, Lord,
    though dutifully offering our best to you,
    we nevertheless want to trust that all will be well.
Instead, as we look up to heaven,
    we see the Lamb of God, again and again.
Jehovah Jireh,
    our insufficiency is made perfect by the violent death of your Beloved Son.
Our inefficiency is made whole
    by the joyful obedience of your Beloved.
You will bless those who walk with you
    on this path of not withholding their only beloved,
    but trusting that in giving, we receive all the more,
    in sharing, we are fed,
    in feeding, we are supported.
For in dying, we will be raised to new life,
    in breaking, we partake of wholeness,
    in tearing down, we build a new tabernacle,
    and in surrendering, we are being held captive by your love.
For your sake we pray. Amen!

Jacob's Ladder

(Genesis 28, 32)

"Surely the LORD is in this place—and I did not know it!" (Gen 28:16).

Be with us, Lord,
    and keep us in all places you lead us to.
"Surely the LORD is in this place,"
    and often we know it not;
    forgive us for being too slow in knowing your presence.
Forgive us for being too timid to wrestle with your angels,
    fearful of asking hard questions,
    and many times too quick to retreat to despair or comfort.

We call upon you all night, O Lord, wrestling with you;
    We will not let you go, unless you bless us.
We have striven with you at the Peniel of our lives,
    "For I have seen God face to face,
    and yet my life is preserved" (Gen 32:30).
    Be merciful to us, Lord!
May you bring us to the House of God,
    Bethel in our pilgrimage,
    for you and you alone are our God. Amen!

To Taste Your Goodness

(Genesis 48–50)

"But his father refused, and said, 'I know, my son, I know; he [Ephraim] also shall become a people, and he also shall be great'" (Gen 48:19).

May our lives not be a threat to others, Lord,
  for we all belong to you.
May the hurt and harm that come our way become blessing and sweetness;
  for Lord, you intended all for good,
  despite what ill intentions others might have for us.
Your sovereign love creates and preserves,
  and through strangers as well as enemies,
  you provide for our needs.
May we live to taste your goodness,
  to see your glory,
  to know of your shepherding us; for the sake of Christ, Amen!

The Great I AM

(Exodus 3)

"The LORD, the God of the Hebrews, has met with us" (Exod 3:18).

God of I AM,
    you are who YOU ARE,
    the eternally Triune God of Father, Son, and Holy Spirit,
    blessed be YOU,
    for you have revealed yourself to us.
Help us to draw near to YOU, Lord,
    that we might behold your glory and live,
    live in trusting obedience of the call to be your servants.
You have heard the cry of your people,
    and in the greater passion of the Cross,
    you have redeemed our sins.
You have known the misery of your people,
    and in the greater pain of Gethsemane,
    you have endured for our pain.
You have seen the suffering of your people,
    and in the greater persecution of the empire,
    you will dethrone all, for you are the Lord of lords. Amen!

Your Holy Name

(Exodus 19–20)

"The whole earth is mine, but you shall be for me a priestly kingdom and a holy nation" (Exod 19:5–6).

Holy Lord, all are yours and you have made a covenant with us,
    making us a priestly people and a holy nation.
You will bless us to bless others,
    you call us to call more.
You beckon us to hear your voice,
    to obey your word, so that we might live.
Draw us to your side,
    that we might fear your holy presence.

You are the Lord our God
    who delivers us from slavery,
    help us to stay in freedom,
    and liberate those who are oppressed.

Strengthen us not to recoil in fear,
    not to make idols out of our insecurity,
    worshipping things and persons—giving them, rather than you, the central place in our lives,
    for you are a jealous God,
    a faithful God whose steadfast love endures forever.
Sensitize us not to be deceiving of ourselves and of your Holy Name,
    help us to glorify your Name and all of creation that you have made covenant with,
    so that all will be redeemed to reflect your glory.

Make us to observe the Sabbath,
and to respect time and place as sacred in our routines and pilgrimage,
so that we might know the original intent
and destiny of being children of God,
finding the source and *telos* of being human is to know you.
Remind us to honor our fathers and mothers,
so that our days may be long in the land,
and gather wisdom for our younger generations.

Help us to remember life as your creative principle always,
that death and murder violate that principle.
Lead us not into temptation,
especially hurting others and their properties,
bearing false witness against our neighbors,
and coveting their belongings.
You are the Lord our God,
save us to be your people who reflect who you are. Amen!

Your Presence

(Exodus 33–34)

"My presence will go with you and I will give you rest" (Exod 33:14).

Thank you for that promise, Lord!
When tasks loom large,
    chores unending,
    and burdens too heavy to carry,
    your presence will carry us through.
When injustice bursts like a volcano,
    violence roars like thunder,
    and temptation pulls us like a magnet,
    your presence will grant us wisdom to stand firm,
    not to give in,
    but to abide in your strength.
Your peace has made us whole,
Your love made us secure,
Your joy made us calm,
And your rest made us trusting you for all.

You are merciful God,
    steadfast in forgiving us,
    slow to anger for our sins.
Despite our disobedience and unbelief,
    reveal yourself to us, Lord.
Speak to us your commandments,
    for without them we are lost,
    by them you led us to freedom.

Nevertheless, you have made us righteous,
    not by what we have done,
    but by your faithfulness.
Unveil yourself to us, Lord,
    that we might find favor in your sight.
We pray that your glory will shine in our midst,
    as we reflect on who you are, our Lord and our God. Amen!

You Are Our Hiding Place[1]

(Psalms 30–32)

"You are a hiding place for me . . ." (Ps 32:7).

Lord,
your anger is but for a moment;
your favor is for a lifetime.
Weeping may tarry for the night,
but joy comes in the morning.
As for me,
I pray for your blessings,
and may I not be moved.
Be with all who come to the seminar this Sunday,
may your Spirit move among them at the Kenyalang Cinema
may your Word be spoken
and may you touch the hearts of many, for the sake of your Name.
God of Truth, have mercy on me,
so that my life will not be spent in sighing,
my years not in distress.
You are my Rock and my Fortress,
save me and guide me.
Lord, I hide not my sins,
for you have known them and have mercy on me.
You are my hiding place;
you will preserve me from trouble;
you will compass me about with songs of deliverance.
May your Name be glorified in the "life seminar." Amen!

1. I prayed this prayer for strength and wisdom as I spoke to an audience of 1,300 people at Kenyalang Park, Kuching, my hometown (in Sarawak, Malaysia), on "Peace/Shalom in Vicissitudes of Life." The seminar was organized by the *Sin Chew Daily* newspaper (Kuching, Sarawak, Malaysia), on July 27, 2003.

Make Glad the City of God

(Psalms 46–54)

Leader [L]: There is a river whose streams make glad the city of God, the holy dwelling of the Most High;

Congregation [C]: **and there we find you as our refuge and our light.**

L: Clap our hands and we will shout unto you,

C: **for you are the King of the earth.**

L: We will think of your steadfastness in your temple, this is your holy mountain,

C: **beautiful in its elevation, and there is joy on all the earth.**

L: Mortals cannot abide in their vanity;

C: **you alone are our anchor and trust, Lord.**

L: We call on you, Lord, in the days of trouble, and pray you will deliver us.

C: **O Lord, create in us a new heart, put a new and steadfast spirit within us.**

L: Restore to us the joy of your salvation, and sustain in us a willing spirit.

C: **We seek your face, O Lord, for your steadfast love is what we count.**

L: Teach us the wisdom of knowing you and rejoicing in your salvation.

C: **Thank you, Lord, for being our helper and the upholder of our lives.**

All: **Praise be to you! Amen!**

Crown Our Years with Your Bounty

(Psalms 66–71)

Leader [L]: You crown our years with your bounty,
Congregation [C]: **we make a joyful noise to you.**

L: How awesome are your deeds,
C: **all the earth worships you.**
L: We come to you and we fear you, Lord;
C: **for you are the God who listens and forgives.**
L: Blessed are you, for you have not rejected our prayers,
C: **but you are steadfast in loving us.**
L: May you be gracious to us,
C: **and make your face to shine upon us.**
L: Teach us to praise you
C: **and revere you from the depths of our hearts.**
L: Awesome are you in your sanctuary,
C: **grant us strength that we may be well, Lord.**
L: Heal us, that we may serve you with joy!
C: **Save us and keep us in your path,**
L: shower your steadfast love upon us.
All: **You are our help and our refuge, the rock of our salvation.**
Our praise to you be continuously in our lives! Amen!

Delighting in Your Holiness

(Psalms 101–110)

"I will sing of loyalty and of justice; to you, O LORD, I will sing" (Ps 101:1).

Purify me, Lord,
that I may delight in your holiness and your law.
Strengthen me,
that I may walk in your righteousness.
Be merciful,
that I may not perish, for your grace is the only joy I have.
People will wear out like garments,
but you are enthroned forever.
Guide and protect all those who lift up their voices to you, Lord.
Have mercy on us.

As the heavens are high above the earth,
so great is your steadfast love toward those who fear you;
as far as the east is from the west,
so far you remove my transgressions from me.
May my meditation be pleasing to you,
my praise be acceptable to you.
Teach me to keep your statutes,
above all, to love you.

Remember me, O Lord,
when you show favor to your people.
Your steadfast love endures forever,
and in it I yearn to live for you, O Lord.

O Holy One, who is priest according to the order of Melchizedek,
    I look to you for mercy,
    that I may labor in your vineyard with care and joy.
Lift up my head,
    that I may look to you for help! Amen!

In the Strange Land[2]

(Psalm 131–140)

"I do not occupy myself with things too great and too marvelous for me" (Ps 131:1).

I have calmed and quieted my soul in you,
    my God and my Comforter.
You have chosen us to be your agents,
    you have blessed us to be your beloved. Alleluia!
    May your favor remain with your people.
How very good and pleasant it is
    when kindred live together in unity,
    for you have blessed us of life forever.
You are the maker of heaven and earth,
    you do whatever pleases you,
    not like idols who are helpless.
    Yet you are merciful. Alleluia!
O, we give thanks to you,
    for your love endures forever.
Lead me to China and back safely,
    and bless my ministry there for your Name's sake.
In the foreign land, I sing your song.
    along the raging rivers, I proclaim your peace, O Lord.
I will give you my whole heart, Lord.
    Help me to walk humbly with you, for you are merciful.
Your knowledge of me is too wonderful,
    and your thought is too high.
I am wonderfully created in your image,
    that I may live imitating your goodness. Alleluia! Amen!

2. I wrote this prayer for faith and strength (in July 2006) as I served as the academic director to administer the Christian Studies programs at Peking University.

Singing a New Song

(Psalms 141–150)

"Let my prayer be counted as incense before you, and the lifting up of my hands as an evening sacrifice" (Ps 141:2).

I look to you, Lord,
  for wisdom and guidance.
When my spirit is overwhelmed within me,
  you know and you release me to glorify you.
Teach me to do your will,
  your Spirit is good.
I will sing a new song unto you, O Lord,
  and pray that our children shall be as plants grown up in their youth.
I wait for you, O Lord,
  that you may embrace me in your care.
Your kingdom is everlasting,
  and you preserve all that love you.
Lord, I will not put my trust in princes and wealth,
  but in you, the Great Jehovah, alone.
You preserve the sojourners and protect the weak.
  May you reign forever.
Show your word to me, O Lord, your statutes and your commandments,
  that I may live in freedom.
Lord, all the creatures of the earth praise you,
  you are great and to be praised. Amen!

Word of Life

(Isaiah 8)

"I will wait for the LORD, who is hiding his face from the house of Jacob, and I will hope in him" (Isa 8:17).

Speak to us, Lord,
    even when our ears are full of wax.
Be gentle with us,
    when our hearts are hard as rocks and dull as ashes.
Have mercy on us,
    when we inflict hardship upon the weak and the weary ones.
Teach us to love you,
    that we might love your own.
Lead us to the Cross,
    that we might know what is faithfulness.
Bathe us with your Word of life
    that we may live in the resurrection power of your utterance. Amen!

The Rock Will Crack for Joy

(Isaiah 55–56)

"Ho, everyone who thirsts, come to the waters . . ." (Isa 55:1).

Remember not our disobedience,
but forget not the covenant you have made with us,
the everlasting sign of your faithfulness.
Call the nations that do not know you, especially my homeland,
because you are the Maker of all.
Your eyes see not an "axis of evil," but mercy;
without your compassion,
we are like mist that evaporates in the blinking of an eye.
For your thoughts are not our thoughts,
nor are our ways your ways, Lord.
For as the heavens are higher than the earth,
so are your ways higher than our ways.

Lord, we live by your Word alone;
your Word will accomplish that which you purpose,
and succeed in the thing for which you sent it.
If we do not seek and praise you,
the rock will crack for joy,
and the mountains and the hills will burst into song.
Blessed are we who trust
in the crucifixion and resurrection of your Son.
Mortal are we,
but mortal was your Son incarnated,
to show us your undying love.
Yet, death conquers him not,
for your power of love defeats death,
and life everlasting is your gift to us all. Amen!

Our Lord, Come . . .

(Isaiah 60)

"Arise, shine; for your light has come, and the glory of the LORD has risen upon you" (Isa 60:1).

"Marana tha [Our LORD, Come]!" (1 Cor 16:22).

Come, Lord, as you breathe unto us life,
that as your children
we may be thankful for your goodness and gift—that is, your Spirit.
Come, Lord, as you speak to us,
that as people created in your image,
we may be honored and called to be bearers of your glory.
Come, Lord, as you accompany us through wilderness,
that as your chosen ones,
we may be led by the pillars of cloud and fire, and find rest as pilgrims without a homeland.
Come, Lord in the person of Jesus Christ,
who touches us with truth and grace
and moves us with your undying love.
Come, Lord, in the presence of the bread and wine,
that you may take and break these common elements, bless and give them to us,
so that your gathered ones around this table may be your body and blood for the world.
O Gracious Lord,
pursue us with your mercy when we wander off;
seek us out with your wisdom when we deceive you and fool ourselves;
cover us with your majesty when we hide our shame from you.

Accept the offerings of our praise, our intellect, our bodies,
but all the more transform them in accordance to your will,
that which is beautiful, perfect, good.
Come, Lord Jesus! Amen!

Why, Lord?

(Job 2–3, 5)

The poor have hope, and injustice shuts its mouth" (Job 5:16).

Almighty Creator,
how we wish to be assured of your power
when the breath of life almost perishes in us.
Merciful One,
how we wish to know that you care,
when we are deserted by all, including you.
All-Knowing One,
how we wish to count on your wisdom
when evil and suffering in the world seem to triumph over your goodness and righteousness.
We wish to know the cause and effect,
thinking that logic is the key to paradise.
We thank you for friends and foes,
not because they provide solutions to our problems,
but because they do care.
We thank you for not providing the answer,
but questions that draw us into your elusive presence.
You have not silenced us with discussion and pursuit of answers,
you have drawn us close to you
by opening up the way of trust and gratitude.
Yes, the "LORD is merciful and compassionate" (James 5:11).

To you and you alone, El Shaddai,
we will seek.
For you do "great and unsearchable things,
marvelous things without number" (Job 5:9).

"You save the needy from the sword of their mouths,
    from the hand of the mighty.
So the poor have hope,
    and injustice shuts its mouth" (Job 5:15–16). Amen!

I Know That My Redeemer Lives

(Job 19)

"For I know that my Redeemer lives, and that at the last he will stand upon the earth" (Job 19:25).

In times of uncertainty,
    grant us hope that you are the Omega;
In times of pain,
    grant us *shalom* that you are the balm of Gilead.
When we are faithless,
    grant us confidence that your Son trusts you even unto death;
When we are disobedient,
    grant us joy that your Son who is called Beloved;
For I know my Redeemer lives,
    and he will sup with us face-to-face! Amen!

Where Were You?

(Job 28)

"Where shall wisdom be found? And where is the place of understanding?" (Job 28:12).

God the Alpha,
    who are we, your creatures, to question you?
We know not the wonder of your creation;
    we know not the mystery of your creative designs;
    we know not the power of your making.
Surely it is good that you speak to Job, and to us,
    for "where were you?"—Lord, we don't know where we were.
Speak, Lord;
    only then we can say, "Here are we."

You speak to Adam and Eve to protect them
    despite their disobedience.
You speak to Noah
    and counsel him to build an ark for the salvation of your choice.
You speak to Abraham
    and make him the instrument of your blessings to all Gentiles.
You speak to Moses
    and guide him to lead your people out from the land of slavery and oppression.
You speak to Joshua
    and lead his people to the promised land.
You speak to Isaiah
    and send him to speak to his people.
You speak to Jeremiah
    and call him to be your prophet.

You speak to Ezekiel
    and warn your people of impending judgment.
You speak to us through your Son
    and grant us salvation.
Great is your faithfulness and your Word. Amen!

Journeying with Community—Being Sojourners

Humans Should Not Be Alone

(Genesis 2)

"And the man and his wife were both naked, and were not ashamed" (Gen 2:25).

How lonely we are, Lord,
    when we flee from you and fight with each other.
Teach us the art of being human, the art of trust,
    so that we may return to you and reconcile with one another.
You created us in your image,
    we are nothing without you,
    and we are incomplete as individuals.
"It is not good that human beings should be alone" (Gen 2:18),
    so you created for each a partner,
    and from there you created community for individuals.
Just as the yin cannot be yin without the yang,
    so are we the co-humanity.

Just as the yang has a part of yin, and the yin has a dot of yang,
so are we constantly embodying others as part of ourselves.
Just as the yin and the yang combine to form the great ultimate,
so do we need to interact with one another and with you to be our whole selves.
We are our sisters' tenders,
our brothers' keepers,
We are our sisters' allies,
our brothers' supporters.
We are the common bone and flesh of each other,
and there is only one humankind, the kindred race of being human.
We are naked and vulnerable before each other,
but we are not afraid,
because you have imparted the gift of mutual trust to us.
Glory be to you. Amen!

Peace within Ourselves

(Genesis 4)

"If you do well, will you not be accepted?" (Gen 4:7).

Grant us peace within ourselves, Lord,
    that we might be secure in knowing what we have done.
Remind us that you have accepted us in Christ,
    whose faithfulness to you nevertheless cost him his life,
    yet your power of resurrection is greater than death.
If we do well, we have no fear,
    for you have loved and approved of us.
If we do not do well,
    teach us not to panic,
    but grant us strength to resist the evil lurking inside us.
Lead us not into temptation;
    deliver us from evil.
Embrace us, that we might not fall but stand in you,
    the rock of our salvation.
Help us not to be jealous of our brothers,
    help us not to have ill thoughts toward our sisters.
Teach us to be keepers of one another,
    so that through the power of your Holy Spirit,
    we become righteous people, edifying one another,
    rather than becoming jealous and murdering each other.
Teach us to live by faith in you;
    for the sake of Christ, Amen!

Our Sins Are Grave, But Your Grace Is Greater

(Genesis 6)

"'I am sorry that I have made them.' But Noah found favor in the sight of the LORD" (Gen 6:8).

Merciful God,
    be not wrathful toward us;
    our sins are grave, but your grace is greater.
Do not judge and reward us according to our deeds;
    we are wicked,
    but your love is wider and deeper than our evil ways.
Do not destroy us,
    but provide a way of salvation for us.
Do not rely upon our merits
    but upon the covenant of your faithfulness.
Inspire us with your Holy Spirit,
    that we might walk with you, obey you,
    and live a righteous life of the new creation. Amen!

Covenant Maker[3]

(Genesis 16–17)

"'You are El-roi;' for she said, 'Have I really seen God and remained alive after seeing him?'" (Gen 16:13).

Lord, why does peace often slide us into jealousy?
—And in fear we build walls of separation.
But in suffering, we yearn for fellowship, and love resolves envy.
Why does security often lead us to hatred?
—And in mistrust we see others as a threat.
But in disaster, we long to embrace one another, and tears replace wrath.
Why does comfort breed self-entitlement?
—And in greed we think only we deserve your gifts.
But in affliction, we are thankful that your grace is upon all,
for we all share the kindred spirit—strangers or families—
and your Spirit heals our fractured image.

Life often appears to be unfair, Lord,
leaving us without any choices.
We are impotent to see beyond the circumstances
and too weak to hold on tight to your promises.
El-roi, the One who sees and protects,
you have mended our misdeeds—Sarah's wrong and Hagar's envy;
you have granted life—despite our afflictions and even hate for one another.
Bid us to come to the well of Beer-lahai-roi,
for we yearn to see you, our Living God.

3. This prayer was rewritten on Ash Wednesday (March 9, 2011) and in the days following (it was completed on March 11, 2011), to connect with the Japanese living in the "apocalyptic" tribulation of the earthquake, tsunami, and nuclear threat of "biblical proportions." To the victims and survivors, may the affliction pass soon.

Help us not to contribute to the problems of life,
But to seek your strength in finding solutions to life's challenges,
and finding ways to be blessings for all.
Help us to not be bitter and jealous,
but be better and zealous,
in trusting your promise of goodness,
so that our transformed hearts will change others' and our fates.

Covenant Maker,
you have promised Abraham and Sarah to be fore-parents of great people,
you have also blessed Hagar and Ishmael to be fruitful, to become great nations.
You have consigned all to trials and tribulations,
so that your mercy might reign over all.
You have chosen your beloved Son,
so that, by his faithfulness even unto death,
we may be faithful to you and one another. Amen!

Rebekah, the Captivating One

(Genesis 23–24)

"May you, our sister, become thousands of myriads; may your offspring gain possession of the gates of their foes" (Gen 24:60).

Lord, we give you thanks for the best of life
    that makes us feel like the princes and princesses of your choice,
    your captivating creation.
Help us cherish the moments
    and commune with wisdom,
    wisdom that takes patience to wait for your choice and to marvel at your timing.
In making decisions on important matters,
    we pray your will be done on earth as it is in heaven.
May our intention to create a family, a nation, and a global community
    reflect your goodwill of peace, charity, and hope.
We see the shadow of the Cross
    in your blessing of Jacob and Esau, Cain and Abel.
    And if our hearts are right with you,
    we have no fear, no hatred, no violence,
    but shared vulnerability, responsibility, and diversity in one big family;
    for the sake of Christ, Amen!

Esau

(Genesis 25–26)

"'I am about to die; of what use is a birthright to me?'" (Gen 25:30).

Dear Lord,
  lead us not into temptation,
  allow us not to act impulsively,
  help us not to live for the sake of our stomachs.
Your beloved Son, Jesus Christ,
  has shown us that
    instant fulfillment and power within reach are but vanity.
Grant us courage to stand with you,
  for your grace supports us always.
Have mercy on us when we betray ourselves,
  when we sell our right in Christ,
  and when we fall into bondage of self-manipulation, self-deception.
Help us not to be angry,
  but to patiently wait for your strength, in times like these;
  through Christ our Lord we pray. Amen!

Love Freely and Fully

(Genesis 29–30)

"Then Jacob kissed Rachel, and wept aloud" (Gen 29:11).

We praise you for the beauty of romance,
    the patience of love,
    the mutual trust between Jacob and Rachel.
Help us, couples and life partners, in our devoted love,
    not to be weary in supporting and trusting each other.
For if we love with purity and all our best,
    even though we do not have perfection in our marriages,
    you have already blessed us.

Remind us of your love, Lord,
    that we might be secure to trust,
    able to love, as you have shown us.
You have loved your Son,
    yet for our sake, you have given your Beloved to us,
    so that we might know that
    you love us as much as, if not more than, you love your Son.
You have demonstrated that you love us,
    because we are impotent to do anything to earn your love.
Help us to love you and one another with thanksgiving,
    and not out of debt.
May we live freely and fully in the salvation of Christ,
    and testify to the power of your love, that strips us of our fear.
Lift us up to soar to your throne,
    and know of your joy! Amen!

Midwives

(Exodus 1)

"But the midwives feared God; they did not do as the king of Egypt commanded them, but they let the boys live" (Exod 1:17).

Let the girls live,
    let the boys die;
    nothing to do with sexism,
    simply cruel and oppressive, simply genocide.
But, Lord, Pharaoh knows not Joseph, the righteous one,
    and Pharaoh fears not you, the Holy One;
    praise be to you that the midwives fear you.
Lord, you have also made the Hebrew women vigorous,
    for they multiplied to strengthen your people.
You identify with people enduring bondage and oppression,
    then and forevermore. Amen!

Pharaoh's Daughter

(Exodus 2)

"When the child grew up, she brought him to Pharaoh's daughter, and she took him as her son" (Exod 2:10).

She is Pharaoh's daughter,
for the sake of love she cares for the lost child.
The baby grows to have the same courage as Pharaoh's daughter:
he cannot stand injustice, and he fights back.
Moses flees,
and his courage protects the daughters of the Midianite priest against the shepherds.
Moses and one of the daughter give birth to a son,
they name him Gershom, for Moses says,
"I have been an alien residing in a foreign land" (Exod 2:22).

God of the Other,
you remember the covenant,
and notice the pain of your people.
You hear the cry of the oppressed.
Help us to be courageous,
to trust you enough to be strangers in a foreign land,
knowing that it is in our being aliens that your grace begins to rain on us;
for the sake of Christ, Amen!

Lenten Faithfulness

(Exodus 15–16)

"Who is like you?" (Exod 15:11).

Help us to live by faith, Lord,
    trusting not in Pharaoh's military might, but in your right hand.
"Who is like you, O LORD, among the gods?
    Who is like you, majestic in holiness, awesome in splendor, doing wonders?" (Exod 15:11).
Teach us not to enjoy the fleeting pleasures of sin,
    but to share the pain and suffering of your people.
"In your steadfast love you led the people whom you redeemed;
    you guided them by your strength to your holy abode" (Exod 15:13).
The world might offer us the best that can be,
    but we would rather be called children of God than be adopted as sons and daughters of Pharaoh.
"Sing to the LORD ,
    for you have triumphed gloriously;
    horse and rider you have thrown into the sea" (Exod 15:21).

In this Lenten season, teach us, Lord,
    not to entertain the thought of dying in the fleshpots and fill of bread,
    but to learn the discipline of fasting and obedience.
Teach us to know that your glory surrounds us,
    dwelling in clouds and fire.
Teach us not be mindless and heartless,
    but to know that if it is your will,
    you will surely give us heavenly bread and quail meat.
We see most clearly in the flesh and blood of Christ you have given us,
    your providence to us and your calling us to be Christ's body.
May our community, its life and works, reflect your glory,
    For the sake of Christ, Amen!

Your Goodness Makes Life Sweet

(Psalms 33–37)

"Let your steadfast love, O LORD, be upon us, even as we hope in you" (Ps 33:22).

Do not let me die in sin,
    waste away in sadness,
    and live in bondage to fear, Lord!
Hold me in your hands,
    protect me from my adversaries;
    be my healer and friend, Lord.
My life is like a breath,
    brief as a mist.
Do not hold your wrath against me, Lord,
    for my hope is in you alone.
Deliver me from my transgressions,
    save me from my habitual sins,
    remove your stroke from me.
Grant me peace of mind,
    a heart to know your will,
and the strength to walk your way.

By the Word of the Lord the heaven is made.
    Praise to you that your eyes
        are upon those who fear you.
    Only your mercy and justice
        will deliver us from evil and famine,
    the kings' might and military
        will lead us to destruction.
    Watch over us, Lord!

We have tasted and we have seen
    that the Lord is good.
    Without your goodness, life could be bitter.
Strengthen us to love you,
    and know that we are your beloved.
Console us when we are brokenhearted.
    Be our encourager, Lord!
"Better is a little that the righteous person has
    than the abundance of many wicked.
For the arms of the wicked shall be broken,
    but the Lord upholds the righteous" (Ps 37:16).
Assure us that
    the greatness of a nation is measured by her mercy
    and the righteousness of your kingdom. Amen!

If We Think . . . [4]

(Isaiah 49)

"Lift up your eyes all around and see . . ." (Isa 49:18).

Lord, you have called us from our mothers' wombs,
    you have known our names from before our inceptions.
May your Name be glorified because of your servants.
If we think we possess the truth of democracy,
    may your mercy cover us so that we can be light to the world;
if we think we are righteous,
    may your love hide our pride so that we can be your instruments of peace.
If we think you are on our side against others,
    may we repent and behold "the Redeemer of Israel, and his Holy One,
    to one deeply despised,
    abhorred by the nations" (Isa 49:7).

O Lord, leaders of nations may be arrogant,
    but they are not the commander in chief, for you are the Lord of Hosts.
O Lord, military might makes us confident,
    but our trust is in neither wealth nor military might.
Reveal to us again and again the power of your Son's crucifixion.
O Lord, capitalism often makes us proud,
    but such ideology is deceitful.
    May we neither believe that we are "too big to fail,"
    nor trust in a bailout plan for our economic security.
Mammoth reigns on Wall Street,
    while the poor on Main Street are asked to pay bonuses to executives.

4. This prayer was written in September 2008, in light of the many people who have not heard of the stock market, let alone "bubbles."

You have made a covenant with us, O Lord,
 only because of your *shalom* can we live—in peace, joy, and love.
Your covenant will set the prisoners free,
 bring light to the darkness;
 your soup kitchen will feed the hungry,
 bring warmth to the homeless.
"Behold, you will make all your mountains a way,
 and your highways shall be exalted.
 These shall come from far: and, lo,
 these from the north and from the west;
 and these from the land of Sinim" (Isa 49:12, KJV).
Have mercy on us.
 O, you are like a woman that cannot forget her sucking child.
Why is it that the more powerful we are,
 the more insecure and vulnerable we feel, Lord?
May a superpower acknowledge her needs,
 may she not lay waste and make desolate smaller nations,
 and not bring greater pain to the people in the world.
"Thus says the Lord God:
 I will soon lift up my hand to the nations,
 And raise my signal to the peoples" (Isa 49:22).
Teach us to embrace one another with open arms,
 and transform our military arms to tools and playground sets.
We long to see days when "kings shall be foster fathers,
 queens nursing mothers" (Isa 49:23).
You will contend with those that contend with you,
 all flesh shall know that you are the Lord,
 the Savior and Redeemer,
 the Mighty One. Amen!

A Tribute to the Iraqis[5]

(Isaiah 54)

"The children of the desolate woman will be more than the children of her that is married, says the LORD" (Isa 54:1).

O Lord, how can the ruined ones of Iraq burst into song and shout? --
Only dead silence, and no shouts of praise to you in the land.
The garden of Eden is no more,
    heavenly bliss is cast out;
    for the coalition tanks and armies raze the plains of Mesopotamia,
    and the two rivers breathe explosive powders and choke to death.
Fire burns the garden of the world again;
        Moab bombs kill innocents.
A B-1 "God's-eye view" sees not beloved souls below.
    Invisible Stealth Bombers rain terror on precious spirits on the ground.
Have mercy on us for building another Tower of Babel,
    our swiftness and supersonic technology are slow to empathize with your children.
Our "shock and awe" reveals our stubbornness,
        our unilateral attack reveals our haste to pride and prejudice.
Judge not the sins of Nineveh,
    but move us to repentant spirits,
    that we might be spared from your judgment.

O Holy One of Israel,
    you have promised,

5. This prayer was written on April 16, 2003, to remember the thousands of innocent Iraqis killed (110,600) in the US–Iraq war (2003–2009). Although they do not appear in most US statistics, their lives in the sight of God are nevertheless as worthy as those of American soldiers killed in the war (4,287). These numbers come from the Associated Press Online: http://en.wikipedia.org/wiki/Casualties_of_the_Iraq_War.

"Do not fear, for you will not be ashamed;
do not be discouraged,
for you will not suffer disgrace" (Isa 54:4).
What are the civilizations of Babylon, Egypt, China, Greece, and Rome
—for that matter, that of the United States—compared to the wisdom of your Son?
You said, "For a brief moment I abandoned you,
but with great compassion I will gather you.
In overflowing wrath for a moment
I hid my face from you,
but with everlasting love
I will have compassion on you,
says the LORD, your Redeemer" (Isa 54:7–8).
We pray to you, the Sovereign Lord,
that the waters of Noah's days will not drown us,
the sword of the cherubim will not keep us out of paradise,
the fire of Lot's days will not burn us to ashes.
The Code of Hammurabi speaks of justice,
and your Torah reveals the Spirit of a righteous people you form,
for you will give us a new heart.
You have promised, "For the mountains may depart
and the hills be removed,
but my steadfast love shall not depart from you,
and my covenant of peace shall not be removed,
says the LORD, who has compassion on you" (54:10).
Teach us your *shalom*,
that we might live in peace.
Help us to know that you are the Only One
who has created the smith who blows the fire of coals,
and produces a weapon fit for its purpose;
but you also are the Almighty,
who created the ravager to destroy.
Merciful God, we rest in your meekness. Amen!

Your Spirit Is upon Us

(Isaiah 61–62)

"... For Jerusalem's sake I will not rest ..." (Isa 62:1).

Your Spirit is upon us, Lord,
    for you have anointed us to be ministers of Christ's gospel.
You have empowered us to release the oppressed;
    you have comforted us, that we might be forgiving of our trespassers
    and be the source of strength and joy to those brokenhearted.
You have reconciled us so that we might be instruments of your peace.
We will proclaim freedom to the captives,
    proclaim the year of your favor,
    so that those who mourn might find hope,
    those wavering might find assurance.
Merciful God,
    replace the ashes of grief with your oil of celebration,
    replace our faint spirit with the mantle of praise.
Be our oak of righteousness, Lord,
    that we may be the plants that display our glory.
Your glory is upon your people;
    make us to be agents of salvation,
    to proclaim the good news of righteousness.
    Glory be your Name. Amen!

A Tribute to Professor Stegner[6]

(Job 5)

"He does great things and unsearchable, marvelous things without number" (Job 5:9).

I remember this day
    your beloved son, Dick Stegner;
    may he depart from the labor of this world in peace,
        ascend to your presence in glory;
    may your works in and through his life be a legacy of faithfulness and joy.
I give you thanks for such a mentor,
    who has sheltered me like an angel,
    cared for me like a hen,
    guided me like a shepherd,
    and opened your Word to me like the Lord did with his disciples on the Emmaus Road.
I give you thanks for this faithful servant of yours,
    who in his earthly life never gave up hope,
    but joyfully trusted in your perfect will for him that all is well for those in Christ.
I give you thanks for this child of yours,
    and keep him till the End when the trumpet will sound,
    and we all gather in the presence of our glorious Lord,
    when the sea of suffering will be no more.
Keep us all in faith, hope, and love,
    till the we feast with you at the Messianic banquet, Amen!

6. At the Eucharistic funeral Service of Professor William Richard Stegner (January 9, 2003), this prayer was spoken to express my gratitude for his mentorship and friendship.

JOURNEYING WITH CREATION—*SHALOM* OF THE EARTH IN COEXISTENCE

Let There Be . . .

(Genesis 1)

"God said, 'Let there be . . .'" (Gen 1:3, 6, 9, 11, 14, 20, 24, 26, 28).

Let there be light, Lord,
    that we may see a glimpse of your glory.
Let there be day,
    that we may work and enjoy your goodness.
Let there be night,
    that we may rest and delight in each other's company.
Let there be sky,
    that we may soar into your presence with our minds.
Let there be sun, moon, and stars,
    that we may know your wondrous power.
Let there be land,
    that we may dwell in peace on earth and live with goodwill towards all.

Let there be vegetation,
that we may be nurtured by the abundance of your creation.
Let there be living creatures,
that we may learn from their superabundance and care for our coexistence.
Form us, the humans, with your Spirit,
grant us life and dignity and interdependence,
that we may reflect your image and beauty.
For your sake we pray. Amen!

Walking with God[7]

(Genesis 5)

"Enoch walked with God" (Gen 5:24).

How great and majestic is your name on the earth, O Lord!
    You, who have created the stars and galaxies and name each one of them,
    the same Almighty who created us in your image,
    calling us to be children of God, sons and daughters of Adam.
You, who have created eternity,
    the same Gracious one who redeems us from sin and weakness.
You remind us of the brevity of life, the unexpected,
    and also the preciousness and miracles and possibilities you have given us.
Teach us to walk with you in the days of our lives,
    just as Enoch walked with you;
    then he was no more, for you took him.
May those who perish find hope in you,
    for they are safely home.
Be merciful to all of us,
    that we may live not in your anger but in your love. Amen!

7. I wrote this prayer in memory of the seven crew members of STS-107 who died in the Columbia Space Shuttle disaster, February 1, 2003, to say that the human spirit of journeying to the mystery is indeed admirable and immortal.

Source of All Wonders

(Exodus 4)

"Who gives speech to mortals? Who makes them mute or deaf, seeing or blind?" (Exod 4:11).

Source of all wonders,
    you work miracles, not to make us believe
    but to judge our unbelief.
Giver of all eloquence,
    you create us not to make us frivolous
    but to use us as ambassadors of your kingdom.
Maker of the Firstborn,
    you create not your Son
    but have chosen him from the foundation of the world
        to be the Firstborn of all creation
    so that we might be your adopted children,
        circumcised in heart with joyful obedience,
        beloved as pearls in your eyes;
    for the sake of Christ, Amen!

Pass Over Our Foolishness

(Exodus 8–12)

"'It is the Passover sacrifice to the LORD, for he passed the houses of the Israelites'" (Exod 12:27).

"Because in his divine forbearance he had passed over the sins previously committed" (Rom 3:25).

The Sovereign One,
 our wisdom is sillier than your "foolishness,"
 for the secret art and science of human flourishing
 cannot even duplicate the natural miracles of life you created.
The magicians and their sorcery cannot turn water into blood,
 cannot make lice into massive swarms of gnats covering the land.
Help us not to harden our hearts,
 but to repent, to humble ourselves,
 and to work towards the *shalom* of your creation.
We pray not for another plague:
 we pray swarms of flies will not cover the land,
 we pray all livestock will live,
 we pray that mad-cow disease and bird flu will not break out;
 we pray SARS (Severe Acute Respiratory Syndrome) will be eradicated
  soon.
We pray for people suffering with cancer or HIV,
 that they will live with dignity and purpose.

We pray you will pass over our foolishness,
 teach us to be responsible to ecology;
 restrain us from using weapons and chemicals to harm the earth,
 for we are fearful of an apocalypse of locusts and hail and cosmic
  darkness overwhelming all.

On that day when our firstborn become innocent sacrifices,
we know our wisdom and self-control are mere stupidity.
We wish to turn to you in obedience to your will,
for we know it is your Firstborn who redeems us
while we were yet sinners, your beloved Son through whom you adopted us,
and your only begotten One who helps us to pass over the fate of death,
the destiny of destruction, and the process of nihilism.
For the sake of Christ we pray. Amen!

Our Offering to You

(Exodus 28–30)

"Aaron shall offer fragrant incense on it; every morning when he dresses the lamps he shall offer it" (Exod 30:7).

Lord, you raise the poor from the dust,
    and lift the needy from the ash heap,
    you make them sit with princes.
We praise you for your justice and mercy!
    Teach us to walk in your light and your law.
Be the King of our lives,
    the joy of our work.

May we strive toward perfection, Lord,
    for this is your will for us,
    that we may live a sanctified life before you.
May we offer our best to you,
    knowing you have graced our service with gifts of the Holy Spirit.
May we give you the sweetest,
    for you have baptized us with the aroma of Christ, in sync with your creation.
In all we do,
    we wish to glorify you.
    For the sake of Christ we pray. Amen!

To Behold Your Beauty

(Psalms 26–29)

"One thing I asked of the LORD, that will I seek after: to live in the house of the LORD all the days of my life" (Ps 27:4).

Lord,
grant that I may stand on your holy ground,
to walk in your righteous path,
that I may praise you and be your servant.
I ask of you one thing, Lord,
that I may dwell in your house all the days of my life,
to behold your beauty,
and to inquire in your temple.
Be with me in times of weakness,
grant me wisdom to speak your truth
to those who are seeking after you.
You are my rock of salvation, my stronghold.
Support me in times of weakness,
sustain me in times of need,
shepherding me that I may dwell in your grace.
You are the God of glory,
grant me your peace and wisdom,
that I may serve you with joy. Amen!

Count Our Days

(Psalms 90–95)

"Teach us to count our days that we may gain a wise heart" (Ps 90:12).

Lord, you are our dwelling place,
    where your salvation is procured,
    our hope secured.
Teach us to count our days
    that we may gain a wise heart.
We want to live in the shelter of the Most High
    and abide in the shadow of the Almighty,
    for you are our refuge and shelter.
We pray that no evil shall befall us,
    and no scourge come near our tent.
Show us eternal life;
    shower us with your joy, Lord.
We want to grow strong in your court,
    to sing praises to you,
    and dance for you.
You are robed in majesty,
    and your decrees are sure,
    your dwelling place is holiness.
Establish your work in and through us,
    that we may joyfully serve and trust you.
O Lord, you are God,
    and we are the sheep of your pasture.
May we rest in your mercy,
    and find hope in your salvation. Amen!

Terror Trembles Before You

(Psalms 96–100)

"Worship the LORD in holy splendor; tremble before him, all the earth" (Ps 96:9).

You are the King, the merciful and sovereign one;
　　praise be to your Name.
May terror in this world tremble before you,
　　may the people of the earth bow before you.
Rescue us from wickedness and wastefulness,
　　that we may pursue *shalom* of the earth,
　　and rejoice with creation in your holy love.
Move us to make a joyful music to you,
　　for you are the King,
　　and your reign has reached the ends of the universe.
Holy are you,
　　and abundant is your mercy.
Keep us safe in your love,
　　that we may know your peace,
Lord, you are good,
　　and you are our shepherd. Amen!

We Will Know War No More[8]

(Isaiah 2)

"They shall beat their swords into plowshares, and their spears into pruning hooks" (Isa 2:4),

Merciful God,
    the blast of bombs shatters our eardrums,
    the burnt ashes block our noses,
    the cries of children pierce our hearts;
    yet, tanks run, terror reigns, bullets rain.

Gracious Lord,
    teach us the discipline of repentance;
    help us to turn to you for light and inspiration,
    and to reject the idol of human devices,
        for the more we wish to outsmart others,
        the more we wish to abuse them.
Help us to turn to you for humility and mercy,
    to rebuke our high-tech confidence and military conquest,
        for the more we wish to be a superpower,
        the more we wish to make enemies.
Help us to turn to you for unity and empathy,
    and to cast out the demons of destruction and hopelessness,
        for the more we try to retreat to ourselves,
        the more we approach death.

8. This prayer was written for the U.S. and Somali people when the war in Somalia broke out in July 2006.

Grant us the vision that your Word will come to us,
    your law will free us.
Grace us the strength to serve our neighbors,
    and love our enemies as you love us.
Give us the hope that soon—very soon, Lord—
    we can beat swords into plowshares,
    and spears into pruning hooks.
We pray for your *shalom* in the name of your Messiah. Amen!

That Day

(Isaiah 9, 11)

"For unto us a child is born, unto us a son is given; and the government shall be upon his shoulder: and his name shall be called Wonderful, Counselor, the mighty God, the everlasting Father, the Prince of Peace" (Isa 9:6).

When we retreat to darkness,
    shine out to us your light.
When we are in despair and affliction,
    rescue us to your land of hope.
When we are oppressed by evil,
    free us to your Emmanuel promise of newness.

Rest upon us, Spirit of God,
    grant us wisdom and understanding,
    grant us counsel and might,
    grant us knowledge and fear of the Lord.
Help us to be gentle with the earth,
    to be compassionate towards the poor,
    and to walk in the righteousness of your way.
We look forward to that Day,
    when the wolf shall dwell with the lamb,
    the leopard lie down with the kid,
    and the calf and the young lion and the fatling together,
    and a little child shall lead them in your playground.
Give us vision of your reign;
    grant us peace. Amen!

Your Coming and Your Salvation[9]

(Isaiah 35)

"A highway shall be there, and it shall be called the Holy Way . . . but it shall be for God's people; no traveler, not even fools, shall go astray" (Isa 35:8).

Lord, help us to rejoice in singing your praise,
 for we have seen your glory and your salvation.
Equip us to strengthen weak hands,
 to support feeble knees.
Cast our fear away except to fear you,
 that we might be strong.
Behold, your our God "will come with vengeance,
 With terrible recompense.
 He will come and save you" (Isa 35:4).

Your coming and your salvation
 are one and the same.
The blind will see,
 the deaf hear,
 the lame leap,
 the dumb praise;
 from the wilderness will spring water,
  in the desert streams of praise.
Your highway of holiness and salvation will come.
Grant that we may live in joy and gladness,
 for sorrow and sighing shall flee away in the sight of your coming. Amen!

9. This prayer was written for the victims and rescue workers of the Sichuan earthquake in China, May 2008.

Your Spirit Blows upon Us

(Isaiah 40)

"The glory of the LORD shall be revealed, and all people shall see it together, for the mouth of the LORD has spoken" (Isa 40:5).

"Comfort, O comfort my people" (40:1):
  You have said it
  and we pray your word of comfort will sustain our lives.
We hear the voice of your Son,
  beloved but crucified.
The highways of our civilization will crumble under your reign.
  Make straight the twisted minds of humanity
  and create a place where your glory will be revealed,
  so that all flesh shall see your salvation. Alleluia!

All flesh is grass,
  but your Spirit blows upon it.
The grass withers, the flower fades;
  but your word stands forever.
You rule over nations and powers, O Lord.
  All nations before you are as a drop in the bucket,
  as specks of dust in the balance.
You feed your flock like a shepherd,
  you gather the lambs with your arm,
  and carry us in your bosom.
It is you who sits upon the circle of the earth,
  teaches us to lift up our eyes on high,
  and behold your power in creating all.
We have yet to know; we have yet to hear,
  that you the everlasting God faint not,

our Lord wearies not,
the Creator of the ends of the earth sleeps not.
The wise do not seek your wisdom;
the foolish despise your understanding.
You give power to the weak,
those who are destitute, you increase their wealth.
Make us thirst for your truth,
hunger for your justice,
yearn for your mercy,
and desire your love.
We wait upon you, Lord,
and pray that you will renew our strength,
that we might soar with wings as eagles.
We shall run for you,
and not be weary;
and we shall walk,
and not faint. Alleluia! Amen!

A Bruised Reed and Smoking Flax

(Isaiah 42)

"Here is my servant, whom I uphold, my chose, in whom my soul delights" (Isa 42:1).

Creator of heaven and earth,
    blessed are you who calls us to be your servants,
    blessed are those who delight in you.
Your Spirit is upon us,
    you shall bring justice to the world.
"A bruised reed shall you not break,
    and the smoking flax shall you not quench:
    you shall bring forth judgment unto truth" (Isa 42:3, KJV).
Help us not to be frail,
    help us not to be discouraged,
    but to serve you till your judgment is set on earth,
    and the isles shall wait for your holy law.
You have given us a covenanted people a light to the nations,
    to grant sight to the blind,
    freedom to those in bondage. Amen!

Pure in Heart

(Isaiah 48)

"For my name's sake I defer my anger, for the sake of my praise I restrain it for you, so that I may not cut you off"(Isa 48:9).

We call upon your name in truth and righteousness,
    for you are the Alpha and the Omega,
    and nothing exists without you;
    all will be lost without you,
    and those who turn away from you betray themselves as well.
Refine us to be pure in heart,
    that we may turn to you;
    shape us to be Christ-like,
    that we may reflect your mercy;
    use us as your instruments,
    that we may live in joyful obedience to your reign.
You have spoken from the beginning to the cosmos,
    and all declare your beauty.
You have used your people as servants,
    and we worship your glory.
You have granted us peace,
    and your Spirit has sanctified and blessed us. Amen!

Do You Know?

(Job 39)

"Do you know . . . ?" (Job 15:9; 37:15, 16; 38:33; 39:1, 2).

Almighty,
    you are the Sovereign One,
    neither because the law of moral perfection dictates your actions,
    nor because the principle of justice is binding for you;
    but because you are the standard of justice,
    and you use your power according to your own moral perfection.
Before there were justice and morality, you are,
    and nothing is outside your power.
Because you are the eschatological Adam,
    you are the First.
We know not the birthing process or delivery times for animals;
    we know not the might of horses;
    we know not how the hawk soars,
    and how eagles' eyes are so sharp.
But we pray you will teach us to know you
    and your sovereign love,
        that in your perfect will
        we are also within your care and grace. Amen!

Journeying with Empathy—The Priesthood of All Believers

The Master Plan

(Genesis 11–13)

"Then they said, 'Come, let us build ourselves a city, and a tower with its top in the heavens, and let us make a name for ourselves'" (Gen 11:4).

Merciful Lord, forgive us
  when we turn your gifts into avenues to self-glory,
  when we make your blessings a way to replace you,
  when we deliberately use our humanity to alienate ourselves from you.
Forgive us and help us to behold only your glory,
  seeking nothing else but you,
  and—simple in heart—drawing near to you.
Help us to see the master plan,
  despite your wrath, judgment, and punishment upon us;
greater good is done by your wondrous will,
  and your awesome hope to make humanity the best it can be,
  humanity whom your beloved Son embodies and redeems.

Lord, thank you for calling us and giving us promises,
for asking us to go, and leading us;
for using us as blessings for more people.
Help us to trust you in joyful obedience,
that our families might not come between you and us,
but be recipients of your grace as well,
and so adopted into the family of God. Amen!

You Are

(Genesis 14–15)

"Blessed be God Most High [El Elyon], who has delivered your enemies into your hand!" (Gen 14:20).

Blessed are you,
    God of the Most High, the Holy One of Israel!
Teach us to carry one another's loads,
    share each other's cares,
    and confess to one another our sins,
    that we might be compassionate priests to all.
We ask that you bless us to bless others,
    teach us to tithe our lives as sacrifices of praise to you,
    and to live in mutual openness and sharing as the new family of Christ.

Lord of promise,
    you speak, and things come into being;
    you created stars and heaven;
    you created your chosen people and nations.
You are our shield,
    and our reward shall be great.
You are El Elyon,
    the one who prepares and supplies as you promise.
You are the covenant maker,
    the one who is fully aware of all that happens,
    and the one who is able to keep it.
Replace our weariness with your grace,
    our ignorance with your promise,
    our impotence with your faithfulness,
    and our doubt with the hope of your covenant.

Help our unbelief,
    so that we might trust you,
    and be reckoned as righteous.

But above all,
    count the faithfulness of Christ as our avenue to you,
    so that we might be secured in your grace and love. Amen!

You Will Do

(Exodus 6)

"Now we shall see what You will do" (Exod 6:1).

You are our Lord,
    You appear to us in mysterious and mighty ways.
You make a covenant of grace with us,
    blessing us as resident aliens, as world citizens.
You have heard the groaning of your people,
    those who suffer injustice and oppression,
    who live in sin and bondage,
    and who yearn for hope but without promise.
Free us, O Lord, from the burden of oppressing others,
    deliver us from self-complacency;
    redeem us with an outstretched arm.
Take us as your people,
    for You are our God.
Lead us to the promised land,
    that we may live in trust and thanksgiving to You,
    now and forevermore. Amen!

Our Banner

(Exodus 17)

"'I will be standing there in front of you on the rock at Horeb'" (Exod 17:6).

When we are asking the question,
  why did you bring us out of Egypt?
Lord, ignore our ignorance,
  and bring us not back to the memory of our suffering.
When we question
  "Is the LORD among us or not?"
Lord, do not hide from us,
  and do not teach us a lesson of your absence, but grant us mercy.
When we are in the wilderness of Massah (Test) and Meribah (Quarrel),
  do not be angry with us,
  but forgive us for being stubborn and heart-hardened.
When our hands grow weary and our prayers grow heavy,
  may we find companions who will encourage us to inch along
  the long journey to the promised land.
Help us to war against principalities and powers of darkness,
  but to love our enemies.
Help us to trust you as our banner;
  bring good news of peace and salvation to all.
For the sake of Christ we pray. Amen!

Our Priestly Garments

(Exodus 25–27)

"'Have them make me a sanctuary, so that I may dwell among them'" (Exod 25:8).

Lord, we long to gather in your presence,
    facing your mercy seat,
    around the table,
    illuminated by the lampstand,
    and gradually moving into your holiness.
We long to place on the altar,
    the life you have redeemed,
    so that we might be made righteous by your Son's life,
    and be the body of Christ.
Draw your people to you,
    grant that our priestly garments will intercede for the weak and the poor;
    grant that our prophetic voice will advocate for the oppressed and burdened;
    grant that our spiritual quest will bring us to your throne;
    for the sake of Christ we pray. Amen!

We Cast Our Burden on You

(Psalms 55–64)

Leader [L]: We cast our burden on you, Lord, and ask your arm to sustain us.

All [A]: **In you we trust, Lord, be with us, and we shall not want.**

L: We walk before you, in the light of life.

Women [W]: **Your steadfast love is as high as the heavens.**

Men [M]: **your faithfulness extends to the clouds.**

W: **In the shadow of your wings we take refuge;**

M: **for your steadfast love will meet us.**

A: **Alleluia!**

L: Hear our cry, O God; listen to our prayer;

A: **from the ends of the earth we call to you, when our hearts are faint.**

M: **Once you have spoken,**

W: **twice have we heard it;**

A: **you are our rock and our salvation.**

W: **We think of you on our beds,**

M: **We pray to you in the watches of the night.**

A: **For you are our help, and in the shadow of your wings, we trust and sing for joy.**

L: Our souls are weary, but you are our God.

A: **Let the righteous rejoice in the Lord, and we take refuge in you, Lord.**

L: Let all the upright in heart glory,

A: **and we seek mercy and righteousness in you, Lord. Amen!**

Life Commandments

(Exodus 24, 31–32)

"All that the LORD has spoken we will do" (Exod 19:8; 24:3, 7).

We are bent on evil;
    have mercy on us, Lord.
Do not be angry with us
    when your people fall short of your glory.
Remind us often to keep the Sabbath holy,
    that you might sanctify us.
Keep us in your law,
    that we might observe your holy precepts
    and know you are the Holy One.
Make us dance
    for your gracious salvation,
Ordain us to serve you for the rest of our lives,
for you alone are God!

You have given us laws and commandments,
    that we might live by them.
Help us to see rightness in your laws,
    the beauty of community forming in obeying these laws,
    and the truth that you are the source of life.
"All the words that the LORD has spoken we will do" (Exod 24:3).
We will write down what you have uttered to us,
    build an altar to dedicate ourselves before you,
    and train our people to obey your laws. Amen!

You Set Up Nations

(Isaiah 25–26)

"O LORD, you are my God, I will exalt you, I will praise your name; for you have done wonderful things; your counsels of old are faithfulness and truth" (Isa 25:1).

You set up nations and institutions;
you can judge and destroy them in their rebellion.
Help us to be faithful to you,
for you create justice,
you make justice proper,
and you use your love to replace injustice and abuse of power.
Help us to follow your righteousness.

We pray many will sing a song of your peace
rather than hearing the noise of war,
that many will proclaim your good news of salvation
rather than breeding jealousy and enmity.
We pray many will open their gates,
that righteous nations may keep your truth
rather than moving fleets of tanks and raining bombs on your people.
We pray many will trust in you and live in trust with one another
rather than hating and hurting one another and your ways to peace.
"O LORD . . . the desire of our soul is to your name,
and to the remembrance of you" (Isa 26:8). Amen!

Hold Us and Uphold Us, Lord[10]

(Isaiah 41)

"Listen to me in silence . . . let the peoples renew their strength; let them approach, then let them speak; let us together draw near for judgment" (Isa 41:1).

We will keep silence before you, O Lord,
    and know of your strength.
We will come near to you
    and speak of your faithfulness.
You are the Lord, the first and the last;
    you are the great I AM.
You have called Israel your servant to the nations,
    Jacob your chosen one, that all might be blessed,
    and Abraham your friend, to offer his beloved son for the good of the
            world.
Likewise, you have called us, used us all,
    and grant us your friendship in Christ.
You comfort us not to fear,
    for you are with us.
    We shall not be dismayed,
        for you are our God.
    You will strengthen us;
        yes, you will help us;
        yes, you will uphold us with the right hand of your righteousness.

10. This is a prayer for the Israelis and Palestinians, written on the day I led a group of seminarians to visit the Holocaust Museum and the Sabeel Peace Center in Jerusalem in December 2007.

You are our redeemer, the Holy One of Israel and Gentiles:
When the poor and needy seek water,
you will hear them and not forsake them.
You will open rivers in high places,
and fountains in the midst of the valleys.
Grant that the Israelis and Palestinians will live in your mercy forever,
for they belong to the land that is holy,
and they live in the promises of peace and abundance as they embrace one another. Amen!

You Are Our Light[11]

(Isaiah 44–45)

Leader [L]: You have chosen us, Lord, you have formed us in the womb.

Congregation [C]: **May we not rob our neighbor's water on thirsty land, but share streams on dry ground, and the presence of your Spirit upon our descendants.**

L: We cannot fashion a god or cast an image that can serve us.

C: **You alone are Creator, Savior, and Sustainer of our lives.**

L: You form the light, and create darkness; you make peace, and dispel evil.

C: **You are the Sovereign One; open our eyes to see your righteousness, as the skies and heaven revere and reveal your justice.**

L: May we not strive with you, even as "chosen people," for you are the potter, we are the clay.

C: **Holy One of Israel, train us to be people of your covenant, in freedom to serve our neighbors.**

L: You are a God that hides yourself, that we may seek your heart.

C: **O God of Israel, the Savior, we who trust in you will not be ashamed.**

L: Draw near all nations, assemble your people,
that nations might turn away from vanities of power, oppression and war;
that people might turn away from idols of hatred, segregation, and killing.

C: **For there is no God except you, the just Savior of all, however the state of Israel will be.**

L: We look to you, you are our hope.

C: **You are the Lord of lords, King of kings; every knee bows, every tongue confesses so. Amen!**

11. Written in December 2008, this prayer is for the *shalom* of Palestine, land of the Holy.

Tanks, Missiles, Bombs?[12]

(Isaiah 52–53)

"Shake yourself from the dust, rise up" (Isa 52:2).

One hundred days of genocide
    mutual extermination—Tutsis and Hutus.
Women and children seeking refuge in churches
    could not escape the inevitable fate of horrific death.
The world passes by and goes on with its business
    while the country cries in the flow of blood.
Pleas for help are unheeded;
    the few who want to help can do nothing but watch the corpses.

Lord, to whom is your might revealed?—
Guns, knives, spears? Machetes, clubs, sticks?
For Christ is the tender plant that grows out of dry ground;
    he has neither palace nor Benz,
    and when we see him in the manger and on the colt
    there is no beauty that we desire him,
    neither do we desire to be friends to the sheep and the Prince of Peace.
Your Messiah is despised and rejected by all;
    a man of sorrows,
    and acquainted with grief.
He was despised
    and we esteemed him not.

12. This prayer was written in April 2004 to commemorate the tenth anniversary of the 1994 genocide in which thousands of Tutsis and Hutus in Rwanda were massacred.

Such is your wisdom and way, Lord:
for surely Christ was wounded for our transgressions, our helplessness, and our arrogance;
Christ was bruised for our iniquities.
Forbid our impulse to use violence,
to destroy others and to rid evil.
Christ was the peace that cost him his life;
Christ was the mediator that cost him his blood.
Have mercy on us when we are like sheep gone astray,
we do not even know our way.
Lead us back to you, O Lord!
Forgive us, Lord, for blaspheming your holy Name,
for using the Cross to conquer,
for withholding your love from others.
Strengthen and prepare our feet,
to tread upon the mountains, bringing good tidings and proclaiming peace. Amen!

Naked Before You

(Job 1)

"Naked I came from my mother's womb, and naked shall I return there; the LORD gave, and the LORD has taken away; blessed be the name of the LORD" (Job 1:21).

Lord,
You are the only One to be praised;
  please do not praise your servants,
  only keep us always in need of you.
Do not bless us to keep us religious,
  but help us to know we fear you,
  for you are the sovereign God.
Do not put fences around us to keep us grateful to you,
  help us to worship you, because you are the elusive Creator.
Grant us faith that deconstructs reason,
  reason that wards off doubt,
  and meditation that will bend our knees before your throne of grace.
    Amen!

My Dream Catcher

(Job 7)

"Remember that my life is a breath; my eye will never again see good" (Job 7:7).

Lord, in times of unuttered sadness and suffering,
    I retreat to my bed, but it comforts me not,
    I recoil to my couch, but it does not ease my pain.
Do not allow nightmares to scare me,
    be my dream catcher, that I might think of you and your goodness.
Do not leave me alone,
    for you create so many of us human beings,
    and you set your mind and your Spirit on us.
Lord, visit us every morning,
    but lead us not into temptation, testing, or trials.
Forgive our sins, watcher of humanity,
    while we blindfold ourselves to your glory.
Have mercy on us, seeker of humanity,
    while we turn away from you.
For the sake of Christ we pray. Amen!

Be a Comforter

(Job 16)

"I could encourage you with my mouth, and the solace of my lips would assuage your pain" (Job 16:5).

Dear Lord,
help me not to be a miserable comforter to my friends,
but to hear the depths of their hearts,
to hold their shivering hands,
to stand in their shoes,
and to carry their burdens.
Help me to know when to speak,
and convey the tenderness of my heart,
the strength of your word,
so that the solace of my lips would assuage their pain.
Above all,
help me to walk with my companions to your throne stained with grace,
knowing that we, as your children, are created for one another in your Spirit,
and we all seek your face, stained with tears of compassion!
May your blessed presence and eternal glory shelter the days of our lives,
for the sake of Christ. Amen!

Out of the Whirlwind

(Job 38, 40, 42)

"Then the LORD answered Job out of the whirlwind" (Job 38:1, 40:6).

Lord, why do we begin to understand
    when you speak to us out of the whirlwind?
And there you draw us to listen to the still voice of your Spirit
    as we hear your will.
Why do we question your justice or your love
    when we encounter pain and evil?
Help us to know you are the benevolent Maker of all,
    and you are near to us.
Comfort us, Lord,
    that we may feel the peace when "even if the river is turbulent,
        it is not frightened." Alleluia!
For "I know that you can do all things," Lord.
Your counsel will not be thwarted,
    your intention will be realized.
We have uttered many vanities and much foolishness;
    have mercy on us.
We have not known you;
    we were not keen to contemplate you.
Help us to see you face-to-face
    and live,
And learn the first lesson of theology—repentance and praise!
All glory be yours, yours alone; in the name of Christ, Amen!

JOURNEYING TO WHOLENESS—BEARERS OF THE GOOD NEWS

Your Ark of Protection

(Genesis 8)

"But God remembered Noah and all the wild animals and all the domestic animals that were with him in the ark" (Gen 8:1).

Remember us, Lord,
  that we may live in your ark of protection.
Remember us,
  when we want to depart from you,
  when we are lost in the world of sin,
  when we are in pain.
May you be gracious to all of your creation,
  that they all may abound on earth and multiply,
    testifying to your glory.
We remember your promise not to curse the ground;
  we remember your saving sign of the rainbow,
  and we remember the vitality of life you have showered upon us. Amen!

The Joy of Laughter

(Genesis 21)

"Now Sarah said, 'God has brought laughter for me; everyone who hears will laugh with me'" (Gen 21:6).

Grant us the joy of laughter, Lord,
that we may laugh with you in your miraculous blessings,
that we may laugh at ourselves in persisting in our own ways—with no vision of a way out;
that we may laugh in humility, acknowledging that your way is always best;
that we may laugh at the adversity in our path and know that you always make good out of evil.
Therefore, in family, racial, and national conflicts,
we pray that your blessings continue to be true for all your people,
that we may gather at the well to find our common source of Life,
to come to the temple and worship the only Truth,
and to embrace the only Way so as to come to you with joy of laughter. Amen!

Preserve Our Lives

(Genesis 42–47)

"To Joseph in the land of Egypt were born Manasseh ['forget my hardship'] and Ephraim ['prosperous']" (Gen 46:20).

Great Shepherd of our souls,
    we praise you for loving us dearly.
Keeper of our hearts,
    be with us when we are tempted,
    that we might know the guidance of your truth.
Though we might be bound in chains and wronged for righteousness' sake,
    help us not to begrudge,
    but to know that good prevails over evil.

Teach us to trust in you, Lord,
    despite what evil has done to us.
Teach us to know that your goodness is always more powerful than evil,
    you have chosen us,
    you are with us,
    and you have preserved our lives.
Help us to be overcome by your love,
    thus, we will be overcome by our affection for others.
For you have worked out good for all things,
    despite injustices done.
Make us forget the suffering we have
    and meditate always on your redemption,
    for the sake of Christ, Amen!

Teach us to walk humbly before you,
to let not our youthful pride cause conflict with our brothers and sisters,
for you alone are wise and patient.
Teach us to trust in you,
to let not suffering rob us of your eternal purpose for our lives,
for you alone are the Alpha and the Omega.
Teach us to be friends with you,
to let not our vengeful hearts cause us to ruin others' lives,
for you alone have shown us to how to be a friend to sinners. Amen!

Your People as God to the World

(Exodus 7)

"I will make you as God to Pharaoh . . ." (Exod 7:1).

Have mercy on us, Lord,
    when you think of making us as God to Pharaoh,
    we are your servants.
Have mercy on our timidity,
    grant us courage and confidence
    to do as you would in situations too overwhelming to us.
Have mercy on our reticence,
    grant us word and wisdom to speak as you would,
    that we might sense the outpouring of language.
Have mercy on our pride and arrogance,
    our thinking we can do some things and not other things,
    help us to know that we live only in you,
    and it is only in your might and power, sovereignty and justice,
    that we are called to be your people.
Have mercy on us, Lord. Amen!

Lead Us to the Promised Land

(Exodus 12–14)

"Remember this day on which you came out of Egypt, out of the house of slavery, because the LORD brought you out from there by strength on hand" (Exod 13:3).

Gracious Lord,
you have given us a perpetual ordinance
to remember your salvation in the first month of every year,
for you have given us your Firstborn to be the paschal lamb,
so that through your sacrifice, we might live.
We give you thanks
that Christ's blood is the sign of your protecting us from death,
so that we might live in obedience to you.
We give you thanks
that Christ's blood and the bread are signs of your communion with your people
so that we might live in unity and in worship of you.

Eternal God,
you led the Israelites by pillar of cloud and pillar of fire,
so that they would go towards the Promised Land.
Lead us, with the immersion of your Spirit,
that we might hear your voice and follow your footsteps.
As you have chosen your Son to be the Alpha,
teach us to consecrate our firstborn and firstfruits to be yours,
that you might be honored in all the earth.

Redeemer, you have compassion for us;
  we are timid and faithless.
At the sea we are lost,
  aimlessly struggling to find a direction,
  to find ways to overcome chaos and fear.
But you look upon us from the land,
  leading us to the promised place of milk and honey.
We see the pillar of fire and cloud in the air.
  You are watching over us.
Be with us, Lord. Amen!

Your Dear Ones Long for You

(Psalms 40–44)

"I waited patiently for the LORD; he inclined to me and heard my cry" (Ps 40:1).

Sacrifices and offerings you do not desire,
 but you have given me an open ear.
I delight to do your will, O my God,
 your law is within my heart.
Give me a new song,
 that I might sing your praise.
Let me know your steadfast love and faithfulness,
 that I might live in love.
My soul longs for you, O God,
 as a deer longs for flowing streams.
Do not let my tears wet my bed;
 rescue me from guilt and shame.
You are my hope and my salvation;
 be with me, Lord.
Send your light and your truth;
 let them lead me to your dwelling place.
I will go to the altar of God with exceeding joy,
 for you are my song of salvation.
Redeem us for the sake of your steadfast love, Lord,
 that we may rise from the dust and worship you. Amen!

None but You

(Psalms 72–76)

Leader [L]: All kings shall acknowledge you as King, for you are the Ruler of the universe.

Congregation [C]: **Blessed be your Name, and merciful is your reign.**

L: May we walk in the righteousness of your love, and serve you with purity of heart.

C: **We wish to draw near to you, Lord, for whom have we in heaven but you?**

L: And there is none upon earth that we desire besides you.

C: **Hold our right hands, and keep our feet, that we might be saved.**

L: Let the poor and the needy praise your Name.

C: **May your mercy be with us all who seek you.**

L: We give thanks to you, O Lord, and declare your wondrous deed among the nations.

C: **You are God of love and justice, and you are Savior of the world.**

L: You are the great God who is to be praised.

C: **Blessed be your Name in all the earth. Amen!**

Let Your Face Shine on Us

(Psalms 77–81)

"In the day of my trouble I seek the LORD" (Ps 77:2).

I cry to you, O Lord,
    and know you are merciful!
You wipe away my tears,
    you hear my prayers.
You create the world,
    you care for my life.
    Blessed be your Name!
May we not test your wonder,
    but believe in your power.
Help me through this writing project, I pray.[13]
O Lord, be patient with me,
    that I may learn to be patient with myself.
Restore me, and let your face shine on me,
    that I might worship you
    and walk in your path of righteousness.
Thank you for feeding me with the finest of the wheat,
    for answering me in the secret place of thunder,
    for relieving my shoulders of the burden. Alleluia! Amen!

13. I prayed for wisdom and strength during my sabbatical from September 2003 until August 2004, as I wrote the Luce project on *Musing with Confucius and Paul: Toward a Chinese Christian Theology* (published by Cascade Books in 2008). I was healed of a migraine in December 2003.

Your Love Washes Us, Makes Us Whole

(Psalms 82–89)

"Give justice to the weak and the orphan; maintain the right of the lowly and the destitute" (Ps 82:3).

You alone are the Most High God,
    render peace among nations,
    tender all with love, that they might forgive one another.
For all the nations belong to you, O Lord.
    May the weak and the orphan find justice in you,
    May the widow and the needy find comfort in you.
You are my sun and shield:
    let me dwell in your house forever,
    for your dwelling place is lovely.
Restore us to your love,
    that we may walk in your righteousness.
Gladden the souls of your servants,
    extend your favor and mercy on us, protect us.
Turn to us and be gracious to us,
    keep us in your hand, that we might do your will.
The inhabitants of the city of God, whose memories you preserve,
    sing and dance for you.
In terror and death we cry to you,
    and your steadfastness endures forever.
Our tears roll down our faces,
    but your mercy washes our souls.
Do not hide yourself from us,
    for we will die without praising you.
Blessed be the Lord forever,
    for your wrath will not burn long,
    your love triumphs over all. Amen!

Holy, Holy, Holy

(Isaiah 6)

"In the year that King Uzziah died, I saw the LORD sitting on a throne, high and lofty; and the hem of his robe filled the temple" (Isa 6:1).

In the midst of death and devastation around us,
    help us to see the glory of your throne, Lord.
In the midst of segregation and selfishness,
    help us to be your messengers of service and sharing.
In the midst of pride and contentment,
    help us to do your will and proclaim your way to your people.
"Holy, holy, holy, is the LORD of hosts:
    the whole earth is full of your glory" (Isa 6:3).
You send your beloved Son to us,
    send us then to the lost and the least,
    that our hearts might turn to you,
    our ears listen to you,
    and our eyes catch a glimpse of your glory;
        through Christ our Lord. Amen!

Establish Us, Lord

(Isaiah 7)

"Take heed, and be calm [shaqat]" (Isa 7:4). "If you will not believe [aman], surely you shall not be established [aman]"(Isa 7:9).

Help us not to be weary, Lord,
	but to take heed from your comfort
	that all shall come to pass according to your will.
Help us not to worry, Sophia,
	but to believe in your power
	that all shall be established according to your wisdom.
Help us not to make haste or to wait in vain, Immanuel,
	but to hold on to your promise of the sign
	that you are with us.
Governments will pass,
	but your kingdom will remain.
Evil seems to shout victory in our face,
	but your reign will triumph.
Oppression dehumanizes us and violence destructs your cosmos,
	but your salvation will define the end of your creation.
		Glory be to your Name! Amen!

Live as Your Children

(Isaiah 27, 32)

"In that day sing you unto her, a vineyard of red wine. I the LORD do keep it; I will water it every moment: lest any hurt it, I will keep it night and day" (Isa 27:2–3).

We will take hold of your strength, Lord,
    that we might make peace with you.
We will see the vision of your reign,
    that we might live in justice.
We will walk in the footsteps of your Son,
that we might live as your children.
May we live your peace and know of the resting place, Lord;
    may we taste your goodness and live under the shelter of your mercy.
You will grant us vision of hope,
    hearing of your good news,
    sight of your light,
    understanding of your master plan for creation.
May we live many years of joy and diligence,
    to know of your Spirit poured on us from high.
"And the work of righteousness shall be peace;
    the effect of righteousness quietness and assurance forever" (Isa 32:17).
        Amen!

Shape Us, Lord

(Isaiah 43)

"Do not fear, for I have redeemed you;
I have called you by name; you are mine" (Isa 43:1).

Lord, you have created us;
    you have formed Jacob;
    you have redeemed us,
        and you called us by name,
        for we are yours.
When we pass through the waters,
    be with us, Lord;
        when we walk through the fire,
        protect us.
Be with the leaders of the world,
    that they might be your servants,
    as they usher in your justice and peace to the world,
    rather than corruption and destruction
    burdening your *shalom*.
Be with us, that we might bear witness to your reign of love and grace. Amen!

The Rock Whence We Are Hewn

(Isaiah 50–51)

"The LORD God has given us the tongue of the learned, that we should know how to speak a word in season to those who are weary" (Isa 50:4).

Open my ears, that I may obey your law;
    enlighten my mind, that I may learn your will;
    touch my heart, that I may have compassion for others.
We seek you, O Lord:
    the rock whence we are hewn;
    we want to follow your righteousness.
We look to you, the God of Abraham and Sarah,
    for you have blessed those who trust in your faithfulness.
We look to you, Comforter of all,
    for we yearn to go from the wilderness of Lent
    to the Eden of bliss, simplicity, and peace.
For you have said,
    "My righteousness is near;
    my salvation is gone forth,
    and mine arms shall judge the people" (Isa 51:5, KJV).
We will lift up our eyes to the heavens,
    for your beloved Son has visited and become like one of us.
Our heart is your law,
    we fear you and seek to live out your holy ordinances.
We want to put on strength,
    for you are our Redeemer,
    and we will sing unto you, our everlasting joy. Amen!

Breaking Bread with the Hungry

(Isaiah 57–58)

"Is not this the fast that I choose: to loose the bonds of injustice, to undo the thongs of the yoke, to let the oppressed go free, and to break every yoke?" (Isa 58:6).

Do not be angry with us, Lord,
    for our souls grow faint before you,
    in whom we see the light and forgiveness.
You have seen our ways,
    and we pray for your healing,
    that we might return to you.
There is no peace for us when we are wicked;
    we come to your throne of grace to find *shalom*.
Because we are your people,
    grant that we may love others,
    so that we will be released from sin and rebellion,
    delight in your law, and draw near to you.
Help us to be merciful and share bread with the hungry,
    to shelter the homeless,
    to clothe the naked,
    to heal the sick,
    to comfort the sorrowful,
    to give joy to the afflicted.
Make this community a watered garden,
    like a spring of water,
    whose overflowing water is yours from on high.
You are Holy,
    and we honor you
    and keep your Sabbath. Amen!

Write Us in Your Memory

(Job 14)

"A mortal, born of woman, few of days and full of trouble . . .
Do you fix your eyes on such a one?" (Job 14:1, 3).

Have mercy on us,
for we are mortal beings lacking days and full of suffering.
Fix your eyes on us,
though we wither like grass and fall like flowers.
Only you can lead us through judgment,
and bring purity out of impurity.
Tender of our souls, if you cut us down,
we pray you will also cause us to sprout up.
Keeper of our souls, you will hide us in Sheol,
you will shield us from your wrath,
for you dwell in thick darkness,
your image in us falls wherever your light shines.
Whatever we go through, Lord,
write us in your memory;
for all shall pass away,
but only you will remain—the All in all, the Light of lights.
O Blessed One,
you are eternally merciful.
We will be blessed to be the ashes of your aroma,
and the traces of your divine thought. Amen!

www.ingramcontent.com/pod-product-compliance
Lightning Source LLC
LaVergne TN
LVHW051009080826
845145LV00009B/2539